BRONX, NEW YORK CITY

PUERTO RICO

New York City, 1950s.

My name is Sonia Sotomayor. I was born in the Bronx, which is a part of New York City, on June 25, 1954. My parents, Juan and Celina, were born on the island of Puerto Rico. That makes me and my brother, Juan, "Nuyorican"— we're New Yorkers and we're Puerto Rican.

My parents decided to raise their family in New York, but they had a hard time fitting in at first. In Puerto Rico everyone speaks Spanish. My father, who I called *papi*, could not speak English very well, and he worked at a factory. My mother, or *mami*, worked as a telephone operator. My family didn't have very much money. We spoke Spanish at home and we had different traditions than a lot of the kids I met.

WHEN I GROW UP

SONIA SOTOMAYOR

BY **AnnMarie Anderson**

ILLUSTRATED BY **Gerald Kelley**

Scholastic Inc.

"You've got to get your education! It's the only way to get ahead in the world."

— SONIA SOTOMAYOR

Photo credits:

cover: Supreme Court of the United States, background: DHuss/iStock1; 1: Medioimages/Photodisc; 3: icholakov /iStock; 6 b: jaimax/Fotolia; inset: The White House; 8: fotofrog/iStock; 10 c: THE KOBAL COLLECTION/CBS-TV; 10 background: shaunl/iStock; 14-15: glynspencer/Fotolia; 17: The White House; 18: age fotostock/Alamy; 20-21: ericsphotography/iStock; 22: SeanPavonePhoto/iStock; 24-25: Michael Flippo/Dreamstime; 26: Davidgn/Dreamstime; 27 b: Iakov Filimonov/iStock; inset: Alex Brandon/AP Photos; 28: PICKERELL/iStock; 29: Collection of the Supreme Court of the United States; 30: Timothy A. Clary/AFP/Getty Images/Newscom; 31 bl: Willard/iStock; br: ZargonDesign/iStock; cr: Randy Plett/iStock; tr: Nikada/iStock.

This unauthorized biography was carefully researched to make sure it's accurate. Although the book is written to sound like Sonia Sotomayor is speaking to the reader, these are not her actual statements.

ISBN 978-0-545-66479-0

12 11 10 9 8 7 6 5 4 3 2 1   14 15 16 17 18/0

Printed in the U.S.A.   40

First printing, September 2014

Luckily, we had a lot of family in the Bronx. My papi's mother—my *abuelita*—lived nearby and I loved her very much. My many aunts and cousins lived close, too. We gathered almost every Saturday to play dominoes and eat dinner together.

Even though we struggled at times, my mami knew a good education would help me and my brother succeed in life. So she worked extra-long hours to make enough money to send us to a private school with a good reputation. I knew school was important, too. I studied hard and earned good grades.

When I wasn't studying, I was reading. My favorite books were Nancy Drew mysteries. I began to dream about becoming a **detective** when I grew up, just like Nancy. I imagined my life would be full of adventure!

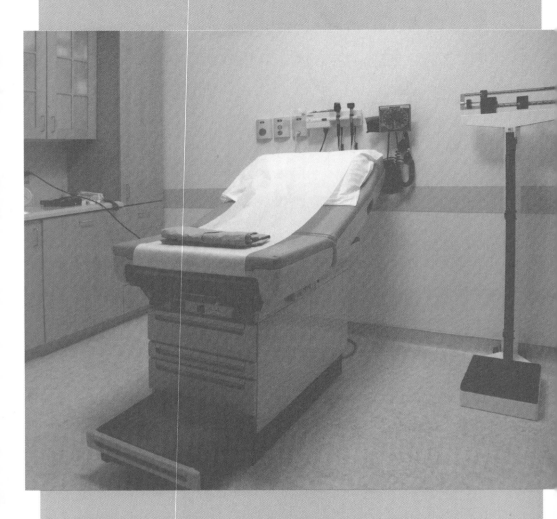

But when I was almost eight years old, I got some bad news. The doctor said I was sick with **diabetes**. I would have to take a shot of medicine every day. When I turned nine, things got even worse. My papi died suddenly from heart problems. Things were harder from then on, but I wouldn't let anything stop me.

My mami was strong just like me. She went back to school so she could get a better job as a nurse. Mami stayed up late at night studying. And I kept studying hard throughout middle school and high school, too.

When I wasn't doing homework or reading, I spent time with friends, went to baseball games, and watched television. My favorite show was *Perry Mason*. It was about a lawyer who helped **innocent** people. I learned being a lawyer was a little like being a detective.

My favorite TV show, *Perry Mason.*

That's when I decided
I wanted to become a
lawyer when I grew up.
But the lawyer wasn't the only one in the
courtroom. There was a judge, too. The judge made
decisions and helped decide between right and
wrong. If I went to college and became a lawyer,
maybe one day I could be a judge!

First, I needed to do well in high school. At Cardinal Spellman High School, I was elected to the student government. I also worked hard outside of school. I held part-time jobs. I worked at a clothing store. After that I got a job at a bakery, and finally at the hospital where my mother worked.

I liked student government, but I wanted to become a better public speaker. I joined a club, where we made speeches and **debated** different issues. I became so good that I won a speech contest during my senior year. I imagined it was just like arguing in a courtroom. Later that year, I was chosen to give the **valedictory address** at my graduation. It was the biggest honor!

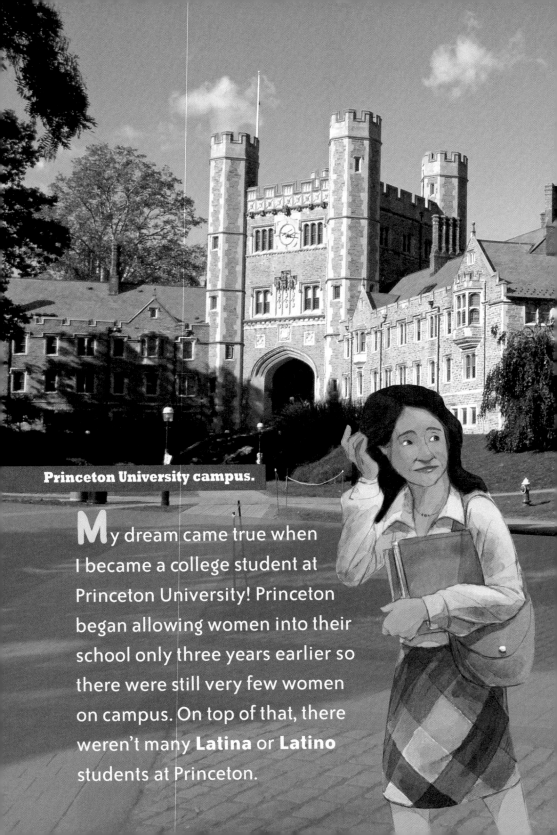

Princeton University campus.

My dream came true when I became a college student at Princeton University! Princeton began allowing women into their school only three years earlier so there were still very few women on campus. On top of that, there weren't many **Latina** or **Latino** students at Princeton.

At first, I felt as though I didn't fit in. I missed my family and friends in the Bronx. Many of the students at Princeton came from families that were much different than mine, and I struggled to make friends. I had worked so hard to get to college, but college was still hard work! I studied a lot and over time things got better.

To make Princeton feel more like home, I joined a Puerto Rican student group. We worked hard to get Princeton to bring more **minority** students and professors to the school. I also volunteered at a local hospital, where I helped Spanish-speaking patients talk to their doctors and nurses who didn't speak Spanish. I fought for what I felt was right.

SONIA MARIA SOTOMAYOR

I am not a champion of lost causes, but of causes
not yet won.
— Norman Thomas

My Princeton experience has been the people I've met.
To them, for their lessons of life, I remain
eternally indebted and appreciative.
To them and to that extra-special person in my life

Thank You — For all that I am and am not.
The sum total of my life here, has been made-up
of little parts from all of you.

During my senior year, I won the Pyne Honor Prize, which was the highest award a student in my class could receive. It is given to someone who has shown excellent scholarship, character, and leadership skills. Later that year, I graduated from college with top honors and a degree in history.

After achieving my first goal—graduating from college—I went after my second goal. I got into Yale Law School! I became the editor of the *Yale Law Journal*, which is an important position. I graduated in 1979 and then passed the bar exam, which is a difficult test that all new lawyers have to take. I was officially a lawyer!

Yale Law School
Ruttenberg Hall
133 Wall Street

AUTHORIZED PERSONNEL
AND THEIR GUESTS ONLY
VIOLATORS WILL BE
PROSECUTED
YALE POLICE DEPARTMENT

My first job as a lawyer was as an assistant
district attorney in New York City. My job was to
prosecute people who had committed crimes. I
had to do a lot of research to figure out which
laws had been broken. I had to gather **evidence**,
talk to **witnesses**, and present my case to a
judge and **jury**. Just like in school, I worked long
hours preparing for each case.

I worked long hours at my day job, but I still made time for the Puerto Rican Legal Defense and Education Fund. I helped educate young Puerto Ricans about what it takes to become a lawyer. And I volunteered with the State of New York Mortgage Agency. We worked to make housing more affordable for all New Yorkers. I was very busy but I still made time to help those who needed it.

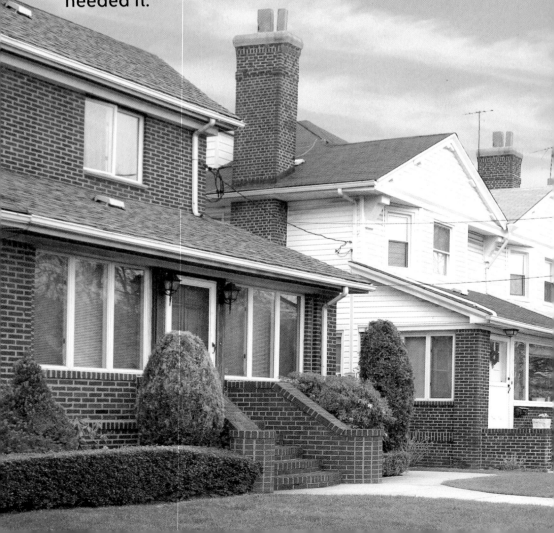

US District Court, Manhattan, NY

After five years in the district attorney's office, I
got a new job working for a small law firm.

I liked being a lawyer, but I still wanted to become a judge someday. Being a judge isn't a job you apply for. Instead, judges are chosen or **appointed**. In 1992, my wish was granted! The president of the United States, George H. W. Bush, asked me to be a judge in a federal court in New York. Of course I said yes!

Being a judge is very different from being a lawyer. I had to listen to both sides, study the law carefully, and decide what is right and fair. Only then would I make a decision. One case that came before me involved my favorite sport, baseball. Major League Baseball players and team owners couldn't agree about how much players should be paid.

The baseball players went on **strike**. In 1994, the World Series was even canceled! In March 1995, the case ended up in my courtroom. I decided the team owners weren't acting fairly. My ruling ended the strike and made a lot of baseball fans happy.

In 1997, the next president of the United States, Bill Clinton, **nominated** me to be a judge for the US Court of Appeals for the Second Circuit. This was an even bigger job than my last one. An appeals court reviews cases that have been decided by a lower court. The appeals court then decides whether the lower court's decision was a fair one.

I served on the US Court of Appeals for the Second Circuit from 1998 until 2009. That year, I got some exciting news. A spot had opened up for a judge on the Supreme Court of the United States. President Barack Obama wanted to nominate me to fill the position!

Me with President Barack Obama.

The Supreme Court of the United States (sometimes shortened to SCOTUS) is the country's highest federal court. Only nine justices serve on the Supreme Court and each must be nominated by the president and confirmed by the US Senate. All decisions made by the Supreme Court are final. Being a Supreme Court justice is a great honor and a big responsibility. But I was willing to take on the challenge.

US Supreme Court Building, Washington, DC.

Samuel Alito

Ruth Bader Ginsburg

Stephen Breyer

Me

Anthony Kennedy

John Paul Stevens

John Roberts

Antonin Scalia

Clarence Thomas

On August 8, 2009, I became the first Latina justice of the Supreme Court of the United States. I was only the third female justice to be appointed to the court. Today, I continue to do what I always dreamed of doing: serve the people of the United States as a Supreme Court justice.

overcame many challenges in my life to get to where I am today. I worked hard, believed in myself, and fought for what I felt was right. Most important, I never let anything get in the way of my dreams. As I said in my speech when I became a Supreme Court justice, "I am an ordinary person who has been blessed with extraordinary opportunities and experiences."

I had the honor of dropping the ball in Times Square on New Year's Eve 2013!

TIME LINE

June 25, 1954:
I was born in the Bronx, New York City.

1962:
I was diagnosed with diabetes.

1972:
I graduated from Cardinal Spellman High School.

1976:
I graduated from Princeton University, with honors.

1979:
I graduated from Yale Law School; started first job as a prosecutor with the Manhattan district attorney's office.

1984:
I worked for a small law firm.

1992:
I was appointed by President George H. W. Bush to be a US district court judge.

March 31, 1995:
My court ruling ended the seven-and-a-half-month baseball strike.

1998:
I was appointed to the US Court of Appeals for the Second Circuit by President Bill Clinton.

August 8, 2009:
I was appointed to the Supreme Court of the United States, the first Latina justice, by President Barack Obama.

YALE

GLOSSARY

appointed: Chosen for a job.

debated: Discussed different views.

detective: Someone who investigates crimes.

diabetes: A disease in which there is too much sugar in the blood.

evidence: Information and facts that help prove something.

innocent: Not guilty.

jury: A group of people at a trial that listens to the facts and decides whether the person accused of a crime is innocent or guilty.

Latina (Latino): A woman (or man) who traces his or her origin from Mexico, Puerto Rico, Cuba, Central and South America, and other Spanish cultures.

minority: A group of people of a particular race, ethnic group, or religion living among a larger group of a different race, ethnic group, or religion.

nominated: Suggested as the right person to receive a job or an honor.

prosecute: To carry out a legal action in a court of law against a person accused of a crime.

strike: To refuse to work because of a disagreement with an employer.

valedictory address: A speech given during a graduation ceremony by a top member of the class.

witnesses: People who provide evidence in a court of law.